D1123244

Mapping the World

VOLUME 7

CITY MAPS

GROLIER
EDUCATIONAL

Published 2002 by Grolier Educational, Danbury, CT 06816

This edition published exclusively for the school and library market

Produced by Andromeda Oxford Limited
11–13 The Vineyard, Abingdon,
Oxon OX14 3PX, U.K.

Copyright © Andromeda Oxford Limited 2002

Contributors: *Peter Evea, Stella Douglas, Peter Elliot, David Fairbairn, Ian Falconer*

Project Consultant: *Dr. David Fairbairn, Lecturer in Geomatics, University of Newcastle-upon-Tyne, England*

Project Director: *Graham Bateman*
Managing Editor: *Shaun Barrington*
Design Manager: *Frankie Wood*
Editorial Assistant: *Marian Dreier*
Picture Researcher: *David Pratt*
Picture Manager: *Claire Turner*
Production: *Clive Sparling*
Index: *Janet Dudley*

Design and origination by Gecko

Printed in Hong Kong

Set ISBN 0-7172-5619-7

Library of Congress Cataloging-in-Publication Data

Mapping the world.
    p. cm.
Includes index.
Contents: v. 1. Ways of mapping the world --v. 2. Observation and measurement -- v. 3. Maps for travelers -- v. 4. Navigation -- v. 5. Mapping new lands -- v. 6. Mapping for governments -- v. 7. City maps -- v. 8. Mapping for today and tomorrow.
ISBN 0-7172-5619-7 (set : alk. paper)
    1. Cartography--Juvenile literature. [1. Cartogaphy. Maps.] I. Grolier Educational (Firm)

GA105.6 .M37 2002
562--dc21

2001051229

Contents

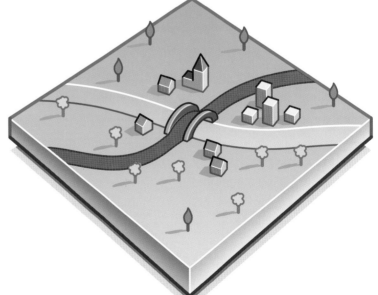

About This Set

Mapping the World is an eight-volume set that describes the history of cartography, discusses its importance in the development of different cultures, and explains how it is done. Cartography is the technique of compiling information for, and then drawing, maps or charts. Each volume examines a particular aspect of mapping and is illustrated by numerous artworks and photographs selected to help understanding of the sometimes complex themes.

After all, cartography is both a science and an art. It has existed since before words were written down and today uses the most up-to-date computer technology and imaging systems. It is vital to governments in peacetime and in wartime, as much as to the individual business person, geologist, vacationer–or pirate! Advances in mapmaking through history have been closely involved with wider advances in science and technology. It demands some understanding of math and at the same time an appreciation of visual creativity. Such a subject is bound to get a little complex at times!

What Is a Map?

We all think we know, but the word is surprisingly difficult to define. "A representation of the earth, or part of the earth, or another part of the universe–usually on a flat surface–that shows a group of features in terms of their relative size and position." But even this long-winded attempt is not the whole story: As explained in Volume 1, most early cultures tried to map the unseen–the underworld, the realms of gods, or the unknown structure of the cosmos. Maps are not just ink on paper or lines on a computer screen. They can be "mental maps." And the problem of mapping a round object–the earth or one of the planets–on a flat surface means that there is no perfect flat map, one that shows precise "size and position."

The cartographer has to compromise to show relative location, direction, and area in the best way for a specific purpose. He or she must decide what information to include and what to leave out: A sea chart is very different from a subway map. This set explains how the information is gathered–by surveying, for example–and how the cartographer makes decisions about scale, map projection, symbols, and all other aspects of mapmaking.

Researching a Subject

Separate topics in the set are presented in sections of from two to six pages so that your understanding of the subject grows in a logical way. Words and phrases in *italic* are explained more fully in the glossaries. Each glossary is specific to one volume. There is a set index in each volume. Recommended further reading and websites are also listed in each volume. At the bottom of each left-hand page there are cross-references to other sections in the set that expand on some aspect of the subject under discussion.

By consulting the index and cross-references, you can follow a particular topic across the set volumes. Each volume takes a different approach. For example, different aspects of the work of the famous mapmaker Gerardus Mercator are discussed in several volumes: the mathematical basis of his map projection in Volume 2, his importance for navigation in Volume 4, and his success as a businessman in Volume 5.

The continuous effort to improve mapping is part of the history of exploration, navigation, warfare, politics, and technology. All of these subjects–and many more–are discussed in *Mapping the World.*

Maps and artworks help
explain technical points
in the text

Cross-references to other relevant
sections in the set give section title,
volume number, and page references

Introduction to Volume 7

Mapping cities is difficult. The urban landscape is very complex, and modern cities expand upward as well as outward, something the cartographer sometimes has to try to record. People have been living in cities for thousands of years, so this volume looks at historical city maps from the Roman, Chinese, and Japanese empires to show how towns were mapped in the past. The maps produced today are not only used by tourists: Scientists studying disease and poverty, and planners in charge of developing the shape of cities also require city maps.

Aspects of the section subject are sometimes explained in separate information boxes

Photographs and illustrations of people, locations, instruments–and, of course, maps–add to the text information

Summary introduces the section topic

Main entry heading to a two-, four-, or six-page section

Each volume is color-coded

▶ Calculating Longitude

For a long time sailors were able to work out their latitude, or position relative to the equator. While explorers kept in sight of the coast, there was little need to calculate how far they had traveled in an easterly or westerly direction. However, as explorers traveled further away from home, they needed more and more to know their longitude.

Lines of longitude, called *meridians*, are imaginary lines on the earth's surface running directly from the North Pole to the South Pole. Longitude is measured eastward and westward from the Prime Meridian (0°). In 1884 an international agreement fixed this line to run through Greenwich in London, England. The longitude of a point is the angle at the center of the earth between the meridian on which it lies and the Prime Meridian. The degrees are numbered west and east of Greenwich up to 180°. Establishing position in an east-west direction was historically much more difficult than working out a ship's latitude, and for centuries sailors could do no more than estimate their longitude, often not very accurately, using dead reckoning (see page 11).

Early methods of trying to measure longitude involved noting the distances of certain stars from the moon or observing the orbits of Jupiter's moons, but none was accurate enough. It is possible to calculate longitude by using the position of the stars. However, the problem with this method is that the stars shift their position eastward every day. To use their positions to calculate your own position, you need to know the precise local time relative to a fixed reference point.

The earth turns 360° (a complete revolution) every day and 15° every hour. If a navigator knew the time in Greenwich, England, which is on the Prime Meridian, or 0° of longitude, and also knew the precise local time, it would be simple math to multiply the time difference (in hours) by 15 to give

SEE ALSO: LATITUDE, LONGITUDE, AND POSITIONING 2: 26–29; FINDING YOUR WAY ON THE OCEAN 4: 10–11

20

John Harrison 1693–1776

In 1714 the British Board of Longitude announced a competition. Whoever could invent a method for accurately finding a ship's longitude would win a huge prize of £20,000. The government was not giving away such a large amount of money for nothing. Being able to calculate longitude could provide enormous advantages in international trading and military seapower, to say nothing of helping prevent disasters at sea resulting from poor navigation. To win the prize, the ship's longitude had to be measured to an accuracy of 0.5 degrees, or 30 minutes, of longitude. Harrison knew that he could win if he could produce a very accurate marine clock, or chronometer. His fourth, brilliant design proved to be accurate enough to win the competition. It was tested at sea during 1761 and 1762, and experiments found that over a 5-month period it had an error of just 1.25 minutes of longitude, easily accurate enough to win the prize.

◀ ▲ Harrison with an earlier clock (above) and the compact design of his fourth model (left).

the ship's longitude. To do this, there had to be an accurate way of measuring time.

Johan Werner first suggested using some sort of timekeeper as early as 1514 but was not able to build one that had enough accuracy. Until John Harrison's designs clocks had to be constantly adjusted. And the problem was even worse at sea, with changes in temperature, dampness, and the ship's movement all upsetting a clock's delicate mechanism. Harrison succeeded in overcoming all these problems. His development of the marine chronometer in the 18th century finally allowed navigators to accurately determine their longitude. By referring to nautical almanacs that were compiled by astronomical observatories, the navigators could work out their position east or west as well as north or south.

◀ World time zones. The time changes by one hour for every 15° of longitude traveled around the earth. You lose or gain a day crossing the International Date Line.

Time Zones

Because the earth spins by 15° of longitude every hour, anyone traveling in a westerly direction will lengthen the day by one hour for every 15° of longitude traveled. Similarly, traveling eastward will shorten the day by one hour. This distance is a long way at the equator, but less and less the further south or north you are. A sailor could not continue to gain or lose time for ever, so in 1884 a Canadian engineer called Sir Sandford Fleming suggested a system of time zones (see diagram on page 20).

He also proposed the International Date Line. This line runs north-south through the Pacific Ocean and avoids major landmasses. When a traveler crosses the line going westward (say, flying from Los Angeles to Sydney), a day is added. Nine on the morning of June 10 immediately becomes 9 a.m. on June 11. In the opposite direction (for example, from Auckland in New Zealand to Honolulu) 9 a.m. on June 11 becomes 9 a.m. on June 10.

21

Captions explain context of illustrations

The Earliest Cities

What is a city? What is "civilization"? Both words come from the Latin word *civitas* meaning citizenship, or state. A city is difficult to define. We know that it is a place that has a large population, but it is not just a crowd of people. A football crowd is not a city. By considering the earliest large settlements, we can try to discover how cities grew.

Maps have often helped cities grow, and they are used to plan cities now. Particular kinds of maps can help the citizens or visitors to the city find their way. These are some of the subjects that we shall look at in this volume.

Cities are settlements in which the people exchange materials and skills with one another and with other settlements. When this happens, some people can become specialists in certain skills, including artistic skills like playing music or painting, because they no longer have to spend all their time hunting or farming. In this way "civilization" was born in cities.

During the 4th Century B.C. in Mesopotamia (modern-day Iraq) farmers built a small settlement. The people made use of the fertile soils beside the Euphrates River. Over time the marshland by the river dried up, and the settlement began to grow. By 2900 B.C. the village had developed into a city called Ur, one of the very first collections of people and buildings that we would recognize as a city, though it was smaller than any of today's cities.

The city became a center for trade. The people of Ur had no stone, metals, or timber. So they traded for these things by producing luxury goods like carvings and gold objects, traveling long distances, west into Syria, south toward India, and east into Persia. The city was eventually abandoned. The Euphrates River changed its course, and irrigation (watering systems) broke down. As the land dried up, it turned into unproductive desert. One of the first cities in history declined due to a lack of water.

◄ ▲ Mohenjo-Daro in Pakistan was one of the largest Bronze Age cities in the world. It was protected from the annual flood waters of the Indus River by being built on huge mud-brick platforms. Houses and streets were in straight lines, north to south.

SEE ALSO: *MAPS OF ANCIENT CIVILIZATIONS* 1: 26–29

◄ The reasons why Machu Picchu was abandoned as a city are unknown. Lack of proper sanitation might have helped cause the spread of disease. The problem of sanitation and the difficulty of retaining a clean water supply when populations increase beyond a certain number limited the size of cities for centuries all over the world. The houses of the 40,000 people of Mohenjo-Daro (opposite) had lavatories and bathrooms.

The Importance of Water

Settlements like Ur grew in areas that had useful features such as water supply, fuel (for most early settlements, wood), and fertile land for crops. Whether a settlement becomes a city is affected by other factors, such as transportation routes and the distance to other settlements. But in the beginning, water supplies are a key advantage.

The Indus Valley, in what is now Pakistan and northwest India, was the site of a civilization that flourished from about 2500 B.C. to 1800 B.C. The annual flood of the Indus River irrigated crops of wheat, barley, dates, and vegetables over a huge area. Almost all the Indus settlements discovered by archaeologists have been located on rivers.

Early Cities in South and Central America

Early civilizations in the Americas like those of the Aztecs, Incas, and Mayans displayed what we would call city planning today. By about 400 A.D. the Mayans of what is now southern Mexico, Guatemala, and northern Belize had built cities where more than 50,000 people lived.

The Incas were a very religious people, and their cities were developed around temples. Temples and palaces were arranged at the center of the city and surrounded by a large plaza, or open area. The rest of the city then spread outward from this central area. The closer a building was to the center, the more important it was; the farther away, the less important it was. The same pattern can be seen in many cities since.

One of the best examples of Incan city planning that has survived is Machu Picchu, built much later than Ur or the Indus Valley cities, probably in the 15th century A.D. As the Incas increased the size of their empire, they surveyed each new province under their control and either improved the existing cities or built new ones, as they did at Machu Picchu. The city is in a good defensive position, with mountains and sheer drops almost all around it.

The organization of early cities required some method of measuring land areas (surveying). But remarkably, though they were good engineers and surveyors, the Incas had no written language and appear to have produced no maps of cities. Despite this, they built many thousands of miles of roads throughout their empire.

Roman Maps

As the Roman civilization developed and the Roman Empire began to expand from the 4th century B.C., accurate maps were needed more and more for building plans and to bring order to the new settlements and conquered territories.

The Romans had a reputation for efficiency in all aspects of their daily lives, in building as much as in military campaigns. They developed mapping techniques and surveying equipment that could be used to plan the city at home and new building abroad. Maps would help control the empire by showing the extent of Roman power and indicating ownership of property, which was vital information for gathering taxes. The maps could also show who was in command of any particular area.

The Agrimensores and the Groma

The task of mapping was given to *agrimensores* (Roman land surveyors). These men had to produce detailed maps of properties and buildings in settlements and mark out surrounding territory to help plan further building. To do this, they developed equipment that would enable them to measure areas and distances accurately.

The *groma* was the main instrument of the Roman land surveyor. It was a simple design, consisting of a long vertical staff topped by a horizontal metal cross with four arms. The cross was attached to the staff by a rod that allowed it to rotate freely. Attached to each arm of the cross was a lead weight, which acted as a plumb line. Since each weighed the same, the metal cross would always remain horizontal. The *groma* was designed to survey straight lines and right angles. That was done by placing the staff upright on the ground and "sighting" a distant object along the metal cross, which was kept level by the weights.

The *groma* was used by the surveyors from around 600 B.C. onward since it was the most

▲ A Roman *agrimensor* uses a *groma* to survey a straight line and create an accurate right angle. The straight roads and rectangular or square buildings shown opposite were created this way.

efficient way of marking out straight lines. So accurate was the *groma* that perfect squares could be marked out for the foundations of buildings.

It was also used in the building of the famous Roman roads. The routes of these roads are easily picked out on current-day maps in many parts of Europe, since they are nearly always in straight lines across the countryside, and the routes are still in use today. The Romans knew that the fastest way between two places was to go in a straight line, saving time and energy. Roman roads were constructed under the watchful eye of the *agrimensores* using their *groma*. The *groma* was set up and another pole was put up in the distance. The *agrimensor* would then sight along the *groma* and get the other pole moved until it was in perfect alignment with all the earlier poles on the route.

This was repeated many times. At the height of the Roman Empire, over 50,000 miles (80,000km) of

SEE ALSO: *HOW TO MAKE MEASUREMENTS FOR MAPS 2: 12–17*

well-constructed highways had been built throughout Europe and North Africa. Many of these routes spread out from Rome itself, and some were so well planned that centuries later railway lines and modern roads follow the same route.

Roman Town Planning

The use of surveying equipment and mapping skills was the backbone of Roman town planning. Maps were also drawn and used to show land ownership and the value of land or extent of land for taxation purposes. This is known as cadastral mapping.

The map of Silchester, a Roman settlement in southern England, shows a well-structured layout, including a number of near perfect right angles in the street pattern. This map was produced by

modern-day archaeologists: Hardly anything remains of the settlement today.

One of the reasons why the Romans favored a right-angle grid system is that it makes the movements of troops much easier—both within the settlement if there is trouble from the population and for getting outside the city quickly to face any threat. The Greek military commander and empire-builder Alexander the Great had the same idea when he established new settlements in conquered territory: Alexandria in Egypt, laid out in 331 B.C., has a similar grid system.

▼ Silchester in southern England, built in the early 3rd century, was a typical, carefully planned Roman settlement. The amphitheater, where games and dramas entertained the people, is outside the city walls.

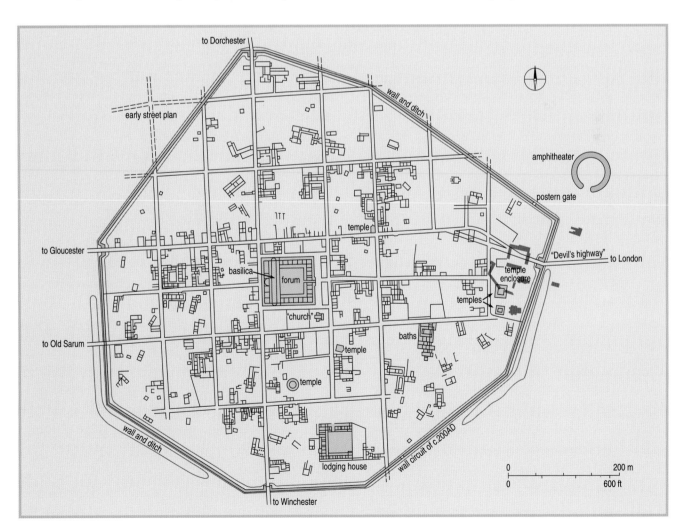

Chinese and Japanese Urban Plans

For centuries China was an area split into warring states. When it first became one huge country in the 2nd century B.C., the first emperor, Shih Huang-ti, faced barbarian enemies in the north and west. To keep an army of hundreds of thousands fighting, he needed money. That meant taxes: But you cannot tax people efficiently unless you know where they are and what they own. It is difficult to plan a military campaign without knowing where to send your armies. Maps are needed for both these tasks.

Chinese and Japanese mapmaking has a long history, the first maps being produced from at least as early as the second century. As with Roman mapping, both Japanese and Chinese maps share a common purpose: They were drawn for powerful governments that used them to control their empires and the people living in them.

Chinese Mapping

Some of the earliest Chinese maps were produced to show their growing empire. Many of the earliest maps use a rectangular grid complete with a scale. China was always at the center of its own world maps, with "barbarians"–anyone who was not Chinese!–put at the edges. In later centuries settlements were mapped out in detail. Most urban maps were produced using little pictures to show the natural features and buildings of the area.

Many Chinese maps also had detailed writing on them. Much of this writing was about the ownership or type of land and buildings being mapped. These maps were then used to tax the people and control land ownership. As discussed elsewhere in this set, one of the most important Chinese contributions to mapping was paper itself!

Japanese Maps

Japanese maps follow a very similar history. The tradition of Japanese mapping was to use pictorial maps. That was because of the way that cartography had developed. Mapmaking was seen as the job of artists, not scientists or mathematicians. The result was the production of pictorial panoramic maps. The pictures used are easily recognizable–as temples or palaces for example–and there is writing on many maps giving place names or building names and uses. This meant that different people could use the maps for different purposes: a traveler, a general, or perhaps a government tax collector.

Mapping of Japanese settlements improved in accuracy during the 17th century. The government ordered the production of new urban plans. They were accurately surveyed, drawn to scale, and accurately presented. The center of the town was drawn in plan view, meaning that only the outlines of the buildings were drawn. However, the Japanese people were so used to pictorial maps that they felt unable to use the new maps.

In addition, the maps used symbols to show the different types of buildings. Symbols are sometimes hard to recognize, and often people prefer pictures (this is a lesson that has been learned by modern-day tourist mapmakers). One response was to draw the main town map as a flat plan and then to add sketched pictures of the most important buildings so that they stood out.

The town was usually set within the surrounding countryside on the map, with hills added in the distance to set the scene. Important buildings in the town, such as temples, would be placed in the center of the map. Many of the maps were colored by hand. Most of them had a scale so the map user could roughly work out distances. Fortifications were omitted from the maps to maintain secrecy.

SEE ALSO: MAP MATERIALS THROUGH HISTORY 1: 18–19; MAPS OF ANCIENT CIVILIZATIONS 1: 26–29

▼ Japanese map of the Todaiji estates in the Ettcho and Echizen Provinces (8th century). This is a pictorial map with detailed annotation. It is not a scientifically accurate map, but it does have a grid to help find locations, which means it was probably a practical guide to the area.

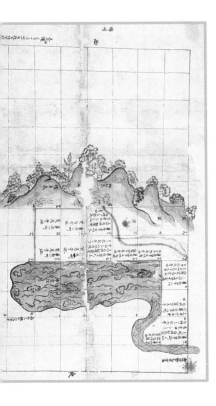

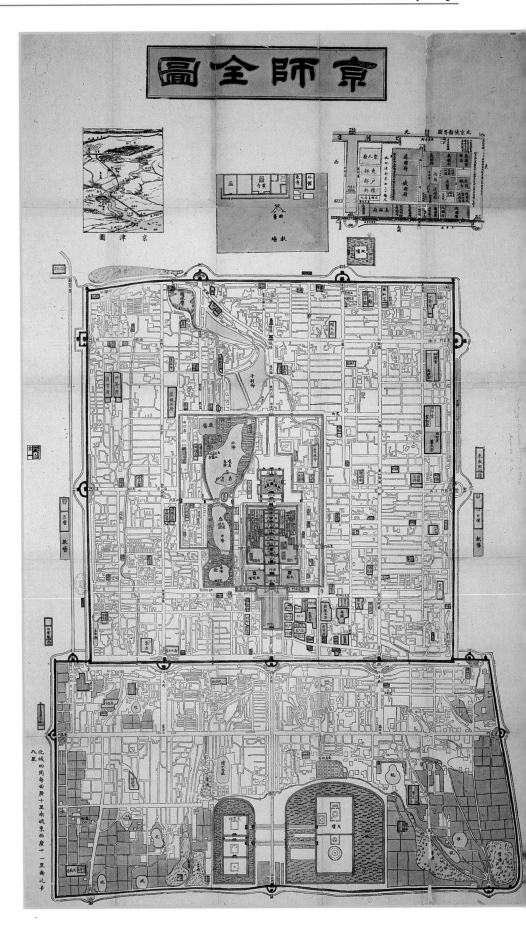

► This Chinese map of Peking (Beijing) was produced using a woodcut template, probably around 1900. It shows the "Forbidden City," the 250-acre royal enclosure colored orange. Around it, marked with a pink border, is the Imperial City. The map is a mix of pictorial mapping and modern plan drawing. The sketch top left shows Peking in relation to the Yellow Sea 100 miles (160 km) away. Twenty-four emperors lived in the Forbidden City, seldom leaving the grounds.

City-States of the 14th to Early 16th Centuries

In 14th- and 15th-century Europe surveyors and cartographers were experimenting with new mapping techniques. Some maps were still being produced using the pictorial oblique representations. Eventually, accurately scaled maps were based on surveys.

The illustration of Venice (opposite) was produced in 1547 but is based on earlier mapping skills. You will notice how strange the view looks. The "high angle" bird's-eye view of the city shows little detail of the buildings since they are drawn with hardly any space between them. The mapmaker wanted to show the network of canals, so he has exaggerated their size. (Venice has no roads.) Had the view been drawn from a low angle, the canals would not have been visible because of the buildings.

The high angle of the view also makes the map more accurate since there are fewer problems with perspective. With a low angle even large buildings at the far side of the city would have to be drawn very small if the view was to be at all realistic. With a higher angle of view they can be drawn to look more like the buildings on the near side of the city in size. (Though they are not drawn to scale.)

Maps as Status Symbols

Apart from helping the traveler, the map of Venice was also produced to establish and promote the identity of the city. It is a kind of ad. In medieval times, especially in Italy, maps were produced of important settlements to give them status. The result was a series of maps of *city-states*. City-states were cities that were rich and powerful enough to govern themselves. Cities like Venice and Florence,

▼ The Italian city of Imola drawn by da Vinci. He has divided the circle into eight segments to improve accuracy. This straight-down view is drawn to a more accurate scale than the oblique view opposite.

► Panoramic view of Venice (1547). The network of canals is clear to help people travel through the city. The rest of the city is cluttered, but major landmarks have their own little sketches for recognition.

though parts of the country of Italy, were not controlled by a central, national government. They raised their own taxes and had their own political organization.

The city was at the center of the maps, and the agricultural land around had little detail. The maps emphasized the importance of the city to the

12

SEE ALSO: *PROPAGANDA MAPPING* **6:** *26–27*

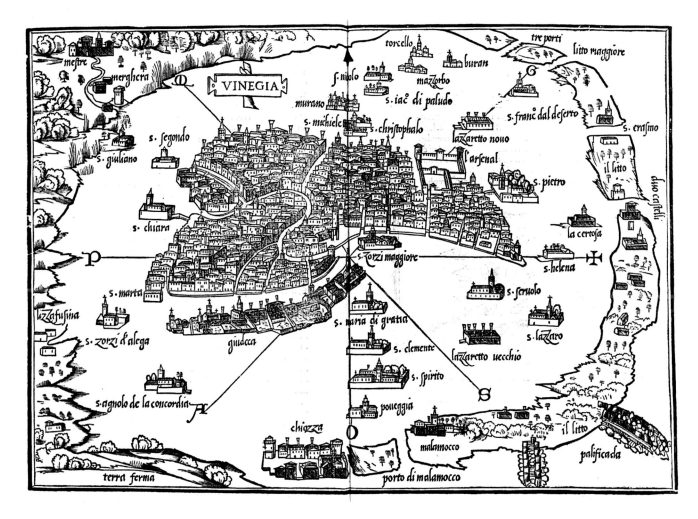

surrounding area and showed the extensive area of countryside under the city's control.

As an important city-state that traded all across the known world, it is not surprising that Venice was a center of mapmaking. Venetian publishers produced maps of Italy and many maps of the world that were revised as information about the New World of the Americas and other areas was received.

Similarly, the city-state of Rome was the birthplace in the middle of the 16th century of the atlas, simply, a book of maps. Before then maps had been almost always sold separately.

Leonardo da Vinci

Alongside his many other inventions and works of art, Leonardo da Vinci produced some of the most famous maps of this time. Born in Tuscany in 1452,

da Vinci was a great painter, designer, and thinker, and he used his skills to solve the problems with mapping that existed at that time. He worked on transforming what the eye could see (for example, a bird's-eye view) into an accurate copy on paper.

Da Vinci improved many of the earlier 14th-century maps of Italian cities by drawing the urban area in the form of a plan. Instead of using small pictures for the buildings, he drew plans of the city layout and outlines of the buildings.

His maps moved away from the Italian tradition of pictorial *oblique* mapping, toward outline plans. He included topographic detail, using shading to give the viewer a feel for the relief or shape of the land. But as shown in the next section, problems with scale and perspective for the city mapmaker would not be easily overcome.

Viewing the City from Above: Panorama Mapping

The first choice for city cartographers is the viewpoint. They can either draw the city as they see it from ground level, or they can try to show a view from overhead. But to map a city—rather than just draw it—from ground level is impossible. All you can show is the first set of buildings in your sight line and the tops of taller buildings in the background.

◄ ▼ "Nadar elevating photography to the level of art" was the mocking caption to this 1862 cartoon of a new surveying method. But photography would eventually improve on pictorial maps like the Paris view below (1871). The fires were started by antigovernment rioters.

Mapping a city from a low oblique angle is time-consuming and very difficult to do. But it is possible to use a combination of mapping, painting, sketching, or engraving to produce pictorial maps, or picture maps.

Such maps are artistic rather than scientific. These maps are known as panorama maps, and they are produced when cartographers view the city from an elevated position and draw what they can see. The position is usually at the top of a hill or high on a valley side. The result is an oblique view of the city and the surrounding land.

Maps like these were produced from the 14th century onward. Many were produced in Italy during the 16th century. They were usually very detailed views of cities that were pleasing to look at, and that contained a lot of information. These picture maps became very popular, although they were expensive to buy.

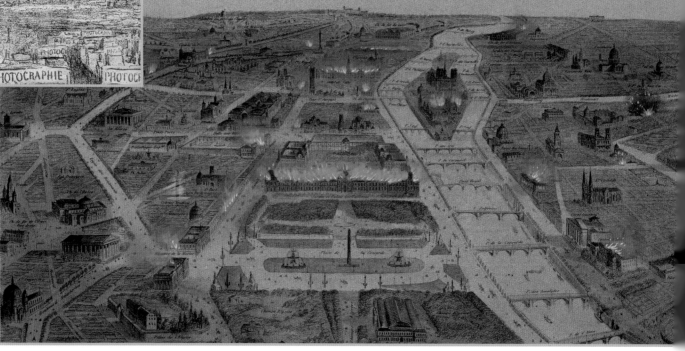

SEE ALSO: *YOUR NEIGHBORHOOD FROM THE AIR* **1:** *8–9;* *PHOTOGRAPHS AND MAPS* **1:** *12–13*

◀ A pictorial view (1851) of London from a balloon tethered over the city. It is difficult now to imagine the effect of that view, seen for the first time, of the biggest city in the world. We are used to such images from books and from flying, but for the journalist Henry Mayhew who went up in a balloon at the time, it was shocking. "I could not tell where the monster city began or ended...in the distance the town seemed to blend into the sky."

The panoramic map was drawn in perspective. This means that it was drawn as the artist saw the view. The result was a map with large buildings with a lot of detail sketched in the foreground and smaller representations of buildings in the background with little detail. Since the map was drawn from an oblique angle, it was not possible to draw the city to scale. Simply, big buildings seen in the distance look small!

The perspective view therefore makes it difficult to actually use the map. To begin with, for the pictorial map to be any use at all, map-readers would have to approach the city from the same direction that the map was drawn.

Viewing the City from a New Angle

During the 19th century there was a development that changed pictorial mapping. The illustration of London (above) was drawn from an unusual location: a balloon tethered high above Hampstead in North London. If you look carefully, you can see that the map was drawn in sections and that not all of them fit together perfectly. It was impossible, because of the wind, to make sure that the balloon was always in the same place when the mapping was done. But the level of detail included on the map is high, with the network of streets and roads revealed directly to the mapmaker for the first time.

You can also see the lack of detail in the distance and the reduced height–or foreshortening–of buildings: typical problems of such perspective views. There is very little clue as to the shape of the land, whether there are hills or valleys. However, you can pick out buildings, parks, the Thames River, and its bridges. The map is beautiful, but like the old-style panorama maps, of limited practical use.

Pictorial maps of cities became less popular during the late 18th century because of the problems of perspective and variable scale. They were replaced by survey-based mapping that meant actually measuring distances on the ground. That gave a true representation of scale and distance.

In the 19th century photographers such as the Frenchman Gaspard Tournachon, known as Nadar, hoped that aerial photography would help in mapping, but his was an idea ahead of its time. It would be more than 60 years before aerial photography was used effectively in mapping.

Large-scale City Mapping

The urban landscapes of the world vary from rich neighborhoods to squatter settlements and from preserved medieval cities like Carcassone in France to modern, planned cities such as Canberra, the capital of Australia. In each case the cartographer has to find some way of showing the structure of the city-its roads, buildings, and open spaces-and give people the information they want about the urban environment.

All cities have a number of functions that have ensured the development and success of the urban way of life throughout the world. Cities provide housing, industrial jobs and jobs in the service sector (such as office work), opportunities for trading and markets, and buildings for administration and government.

In the north of the West African country of Nigeria is a major urban settlement called Kano with a population of well over a million. Like many African cities, it has attracted large numbers of migrants from the surrounding areas, and the population density is very high. Many of the

▲ Chicago from an elevated viewpoint; an easy vantage point to find in a city of skyscrapers.

inhabitants are packed into the old, unplanned housing of the city center constructed from mud bricks. The city originally grew inside protective walls around the main market and mosque.

This central area also has the government buildings. All roads into the city converge into this area. In this crowded inner city within the old walls housing to accommodate migrants has often been built, but it has never been carefully planned.

Around the walled city newer settlements developed in a similarly unplanned way. Many of these settlements were based on intensive agriculture, a big market for food having been created by the growing city. This zone of new development around Kano extends 30 to 60 miles (50 to 100 kilometers) from the old city walls, and its complicated growth has caused problems for mapmakers. The photograph shows the unplanned layout of the mud and clay buildings in the center and the network of narrow passages and streets.

Maps of Kano show a densely packed urban area and surrounding it, unplanned settlement and large areas of intensively farmed agricultural land. These maps tend to be basic, with little detail of the

▲ Kano, Nigeria, an old unplanned African city; the buildings are low, and the street pattern is irregular.

SEE ALSO: *CHOOSING AND DESCRIBING MAP SCALE* **2:** *32–33*

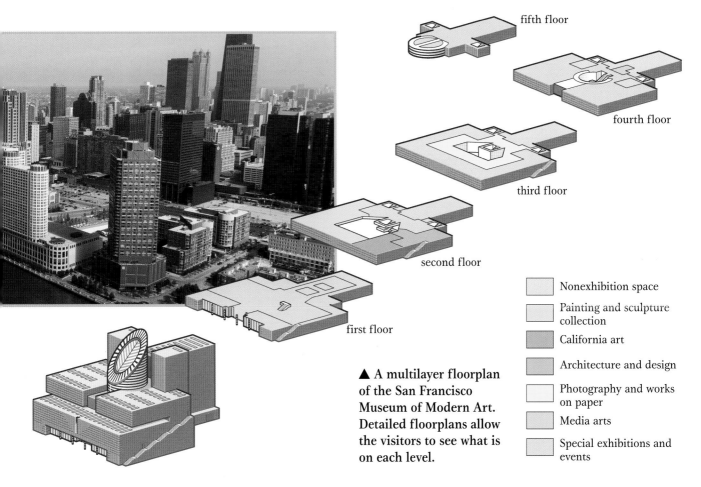

fifth floor

fourth floor

third floor

second floor

first floor

▲ A multilayer floorplan of the San Francisco Museum of Modern Art. Detailed floorplans allow the visitors to see what is on each level.

Nonexhibition space

Painting and sculpture collection

California art

Architecture and design

Photography and works on paper

Media arts

Special exhibitions and events

external or internal structure of buildings. They have to be revised frequently since the shape and structure of the city change so often. The truth is, a map of Kano is never accurate because it is always out-of-date.

Up as Well as Out

Maps of this type of urban area are very different from city maps in more economically developed countries. A map of Chicago, for example, displays very different characteristics. Here the layout of the city has been planned to some extent. Streets and buildings are laid out in a regular pattern.

The photograph shows an oblique aerial view of the city. You can identify the central business district area of the city by the tall buildings.

Land use not only changes outward from the city center, it also changes upward. The mud huts of Kano are all single story, so there is no need to map

buildings internally. In modern cities many buildings have multiple occupancy. Each floor of the many tower blocks may have a different use. It is possible to map this using a variety of techniques.

Oblique mapping can help by "exploding" or cutting away the building and showing each floor stacked up. The diagram shows a building that has been cut away to reveal the different uses for each floor. This technique can be applied to any type of building with many floors, whether an ancient castle or a modern skyscraper. That is something that a map cannot do over a large area.

You can also take a base map of a building and overlay transparent sheets to show its use on the second, third, and fourth floors, and so on. Overlay maps can help city planners work out how much space in their city is used for housing, offices, shops, and so on. Internal building plans can be found inside most tall buildings, like department stores.

Showing Height on Flat City Maps

Mapping the city on a flat piece of paper or presenting the map on a computer screen poses many problems. Almost all cities have tall buildings. How do cartographers show the heights of these buildings on a flat map? Contour lines, or layer tinting, as used on topographic maps, would not work very well on a city map.

The answer really goes right back to the earliest pictorial maps of the Chinese and Japanese. Oblique sketches of buildings, carefully drawn, can show variation in height. The pictorial tradition is still maintained in many maps of cities.

Oblique town maps today are based on the rules of *optical perspective*. The cartographer does not just guess by looking at the city how big to draw the buildings, as in the early picture maps, but follows scientific laws about how light reaches the eye from any viewpoint.

Axonometric Maps

One of the first cartographers to do this was an Austrian called Hermann Bollman. In addition to preparing oblique pictorial maps of valleys and mountainsides in winter for the tourist organizations in ski resorts, Bollman used his skills to draw city maps. By using an unusual type of perspective view, called an axonometric view, he developed a way of drawing each building in the city in great detail right across the map.

The buildings were all drawn on the same scale so the ones in the foreground are the same relative sizes as the ones in the background. The pictorial map views the city from a high oblique angle. Streets are drawn a little wider than they actually are to give the user a clear view of them and to allow for more detailed views of

SEE ALSO: *THREE-DIMENSIONAL MAPPING* **1**: *30–33; VIEWING THE CITY FROM ABOVE: PANORAMA MAPPING* **7**: *14–15*

▼ An axonometric computer-generated view of downtown Chicago. Major streets are broadened and named.

the buildings themselves. All major streets are named on the map to help the user.

Most of the maps produced by Bollman were of European cities, but he also applied his techniques to New York City, where the problem of representing tall buildings is at its most difficult. The illustration of Chicago shows a computer-generated map in the Bollman style. The relative height of the buildings is clear. The key point about axonometric mapping is that it overcomes the problem of perspective. Buildings retain their relative size. However, such a map of the whole of Chicago at the scale shown here would be huge.

These maps can become more detailed. For example, buildings can be "split apart," and locations on each floor can be highlighted. If a computer generates these maps, often you can view them from different points in the city, or streets and buildings can be zoomed in on to see the detail. This is a long way from simple medieval picture maps!

▲ A low angle oblique aerial photograph of Chicago. Lake Michigan is on the left, so we are looking south. See how many different land uses you can find in this photograph: housing, offices, recreational areas. What is almost impossible is to decide what is an apartment block and what is an office. A map could tell you.

Dr. John Snow and the Mapping of Urban Disease

By using mapping, Dr. John Snow, a 19th-century British physician, became the first person to discover how cholera was transmitted. Cholera is a serious illness that still kills thousands of people all over the world. It causes severe stomach cramps, sickness, and diarrhea, and without medical treatment many victims die. At that time nobody knew how to treat it effectively or stop its spread.

In 1831 cholera reached Britain, having traveled with people who caught the disease in India. Many thought the disease was spread through the air. Cholera outbreaks became especially bad in 1853 in London and in Newcastle-upon-Tyne, a major northern port. That year 10,675 people died, and a further epidemic hit London in August 1854. The worst affected areas were in the inner city, including Southwark, Lambeth, and most notably, a very poor district called Soho. Dr. Snow later referred to this as "the most terrible outbreak of Cholera which ever occurred in the kingdom."

During the first three days of September 1854 many people either living near or in Broad Street, Soho, died. Every family in the area was affected. Those who were able to, left the area quickly, leaving the poor and ill behind. By September 10 the death toll had passed 500.

Dr. John Snow was the main reason that this number did not rise even higher. Having trained as a surgeon in Newcastle-upon-Tyne and having had some experience in treating cholera at a nearby mining town, he had set up a medical practice in Soho on Frith Street. From his office he was in an ideal position to monitor the spread of the disease in the area. He was eager to try and prove his theory that poor sanitation and infected water caused the spread of cholera.

A New Statistical Science

During the outbreak Snow interviewed all the affected families and plotted the location of deaths onto a base map of the area. By mapping the spread of cholera, Snow was taking the first steps in a mapping science referred to today as epidemiology, the study of the spread of disease. By mapping the outbreaks of cholera, Snow was able to identify the center of the epidemic, a water pump on the corner of Broad Street and Cambridge Street, which was the main water supply for the Soho area.

▼ This illustration shows a slum area in London, Bluegates Fields, drawn by Gustave Doré in 1874. Overcrowding and unclean water flowing in the streets were perfect conditions for the spread of disease. Sewers ran directly into the Thames River, which supplied much of the drinking water supply.

pump

contaminated pump

cholera death

0   150m

The interviews he had conducted with the affected families all confirmed that this was their source of water. Ten deaths were mapped near the pump, and of these, three victims were children who drank from the pump on the way to school.

Examining water from the pump confirmed the source of infection, and his findings were passed on to the parish council. As an experiment, the pump handle was removed, making it impossible to draw water. The result of this was that the epidemic slowed down dramatically. Even so, by the end of September 616 people had died in Soho.

There were some other deaths mapped by Snow nowhere near to the pump: One woman had lived in Soho and liked the taste of the water so much she got her servant to bring a barrelful from the pump at the start of the epidemic.

▲ A reproduction of Dr. Snow's cholera map. The dots represent deaths from the disease. At the center is the Broad Street water pump. Despite the evidence of Snow's map, his theory was not believed until the Reverend Henry Whitehead helped Snow identify the original cause of the epidemic: Infected babies' diapers had been washed in water contained in a leaking cesspool just a few feet from the Broad Street water pump.

SEE ALSO: *CHARLES BOOTH AND THE MAPPING OF URBAN POVERTY* **7**: *22–23*

Charles Booth and the Mapping of Urban Poverty

Sometimes–as in the case of Dr. John Snow's map–a map can reveal information that can change people's lives. The statistical maps created by Charles Booth at the end of the 19th century would have an even greater effect.

Charles Booth was born in Liverpool, England, on March 30, 1840. The son of a wealthy corn merchant, he joined his brothers to use their father's legacy and create the Booth Steamship Company, building two steamships to carry goods across the Atlantic. The company prospered, and he remained the company chairman until 1912.

In the 1860s Charles Booth read the work of the French philosopher Auguste Comte, who suggested that industrialists look after the welfare of workers and the poor. Booth had always wanted the best for his workers, so these ideas appealed to him, and he became a philanthropist, distressed by the poverty he saw around him and looking for ways to help.

A Map Designed to Change the City

Booth was the first man to produce detailed maps of living conditions and the social status of people at street level. He produced three maps covering all of London, each colored to show the different levels of poverty. His 1889 maps were published in a book called *Life and Labor of the People of London*.

He began his research in December 1886, and he continued until the middle of 1890. For every street in London he collected and recorded his data, coded it, and turned it into a color-coded map. He made observations of streets and consulted records of schools and charitable organizations. He recorded, in particular, details in his notebook about families with children. For each family he wrote their social class and their subcategory (one of eight per class).

Using this information, Booth took an average of the street's social class. He had a further eight categories to cover the mix of people living in the street and the physical condition of the street itself. Combining all this information, he placed each street in one of six color categories: black for the lowest social classes, red for the middle classes, and yellow for the upper-middle and upper classes.

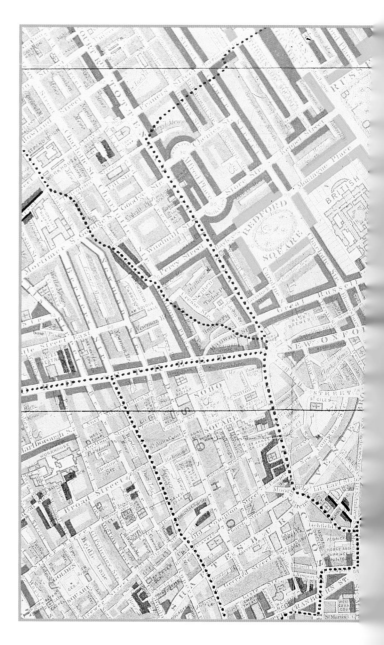

Booth then plotted his data by hand onto an Ordnance Survey map of London. To make sure that his work was correct, Booth put his maps on display, inviting locals to view his maps and correct the color coding if necessary.

His first map (completed in 1887) covered only the East End of London, and none of the streets he studied had any yellow shading at all. This recorded for the first time how poor the area really was.

His second map (published in 1889 on four sheets) covered most of the built-up areas of London and this time included some of the more wealthy districts.

His third map was published in 1902. It was based on his 1889 map, but had been updated by one of Booth's partners who walked the streets of the city with a policeman, recording information in the same way as Booth had done.

The Booth maps, together with the work of others, provided evidence of the terrible living conditions of the poor in London. They showed that 30% of all people in London were living in poverty. It was likely that all other 19th-century industrial cities throughout the world showed similar patterns. Booth strongly believed that if these people were given help, they could improve their lives.

His book did not contain just maps, but was divided into three subject areas: poverty, industry, and the influence of religion on people's lives. Having found the poorest sections of the community, he tried to determine why they were poor. He examined the lives of 4,076 people defined by his own methods as living in poverty and concluded that 62% were paid low or irregular wages, 23% had large families or suffered from illness, and just 15% squandered their earnings or refused to work.

Booth's work was not ignored. From 1905 to 1909 he was appointed a member of a royal commission set up to examine the poor law, legislation designed to help the needy.

He urged the British government to introduce old-age pensions based on the findings of his studies, and in 1908 they were introduced for all old people with income below a set level. This tremendous improvement in ordinary people's lives was the direct result of the mapping exercise completed by Charles Booth.

◀ An example of Booth's statistical map; this is a relatively prosperous part of central London. The rich, grand squares are colored yellow. But a notorious slum area near Lincoln's Inn Fields is colored black.

Location of Cities and Urban Growth

Cities are found in many different places throughout the world today. Geographical advantages–such as good water supply and fertile soil for crops or grazing animals–are usually the starting point for the growth of a city. But they are not the whole story: Other factors come into play as the city ages.

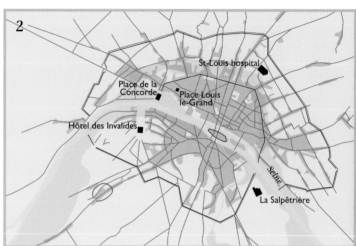

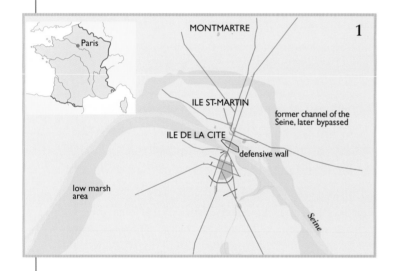

▲▲▼ Paris through 2,000 years. The Romans (left) built on the south bank of the Seine River and the highly defensible Ile de La Cité. By the 17th century (above) there are magnificent city squares and prestige buildings. Today (below) almost all the Paris basin is urbanized.

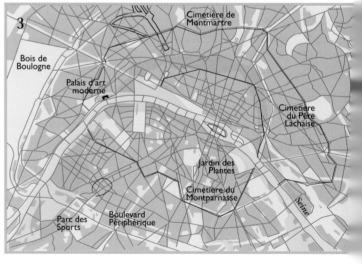

Maps give very good clues as to why settlements grew where they did. A map may show the original geographical factors that led to a site being chosen. These were the natural features and characteristics of the place that first led people to decide to build a settlement. Hundreds of years ago these factors were highly important.

The core areas of many cities (the part that was settled first) would almost always have been built on a dry site with a water supply nearby. Another major concern was often defense. High land or land inside a river bend allowed settlers to protect themselves. Areas of rich soil or lush pasture for grazing animals close to the settlement were important for the supply of food.

Nearby building materials and fuel were also desirable. Usually there was a supply of wood, though some later settlements were located near a quarry for rock to build with. Other metal or mineral deposits might encourage settlement. Coasts, lakes, and rivers all provided a supply of water and food, and were good for transportation and trading. If a settlement was sited at a bridge over a river, it could guard and control the crossing.

SEE ALSO: *HOW LAND IS USED IN CITIES* **7**: 30–33

A map of most settlements shows a network of roads and railways radiating out from the center. Cities that display such a pattern are known as route centers or nodal points.

The more favorable site factors a place had, the more attractive it became for settlement, and the quicker it grew. But over time these site factors became less important. It was where the settlement actually was on the map in relation to other settlements, or its *situation*, that became important. Being close to other settlements and having good transportation access to them would result in growth through trade.

Successful settlements grow and develop their own *functions* separate from their neighboring towns and cities. The functions of a city are its economic and social activities. Towns and cities can be classified by their main function. Most large cities actually have many functions, and it is possible to identify them from maps. Apart from the development of functions, the growth of settlements can be controlled by the *morphology* of the land. Coasts, rivers, steep or flat land, and soil type have all played a part in shaping cities.

Settlement Functions

City functions can be identified:
(1) Commercial—retail parks and major shopping centers; (2) Industrial—heavy industry, high-tech industry, and business parks; (3) Residential—housing for the population; (4) Service—medical care, schools, and universities; (5) Financial—banking and finance center; (6) Entertainment—cultural attractions, theaters, theme parks, and leisure facilities; (7) Government—representative bodies (councils, senates, and the like), tax offices, police, law courts.

Today, the factors for the location and growth of cities are mainly economic and political. Site factors are less important since many of them can now be controlled. Rivers can be straightened, roads tunnel

Confluence of two rivers
Protected on two or three sides by water. Koblenz, Germany; Lyons, France.

River crossing
Narrow point in a valley or shallow part of a river allows a crossing point. Kansas City.

Natural harbor
Gives protection; encourages trade without much harbor investment. New York City.

Margin or head of delta
A plentiful supply of water and fertile alluvial soil attract settlers. Cairo, Egypt.

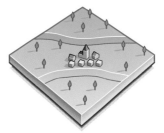

Portage point
Goods are transferred to and from road or rail and boats. Chicago (on Lake Michigan).

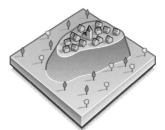

Defensive hilltop site
Easily defended and with clear view of surrounding area. Athens, Greece.

Offshore island
Easily defended, and sea trade routes around them can be controlled. Venice.

Island in a river or bay
Similarly (see left) defensible; passage across is controlled. Ile de La Cité, Paris.

▲ Examples of favorable location factors. Many settlements' first priority was defense and it could be made easier by an area's topography. For most of the big cities in the world—those that are not modern, planned cities—original positive location factors can be identified. The name of the city of Koblenz comes from the Latin word for confluence, *confluentes*.

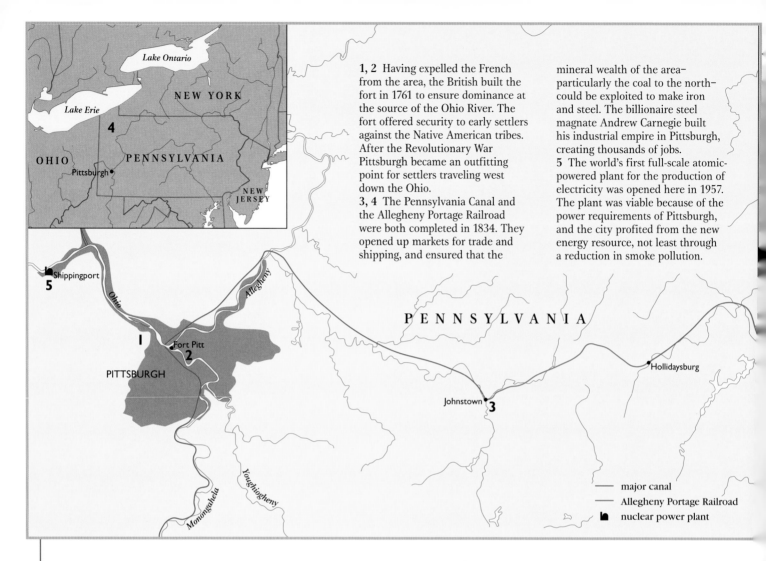

1, 2 Having expelled the French from the area, the British built the fort in 1761 to ensure dominance at the source of the Ohio River. The fort offered security to early settlers against the Native American tribes. After the Revolutionary War Pittsburgh became an outfitting point for settlers traveling west down the Ohio.

3, 4 The Pennsylvania Canal and the Allegheny Portage Railroad were both completed in 1834. They opened up markets for trade and shipping, and ensured that the mineral wealth of the area–particularly the coal to the north–could be exploited to make iron and steel. The billionaire steel magnate Andrew Carnegie built his industrial empire in Pittsburgh, creating thousands of jobs.

5 The world's first full-scale atomic-powered plant for the production of electricity was opened here in 1957. The plant was viable because of the power requirements of Pittsburgh, and the city profited from the new energy resource, not least through a reduction in smoke pollution.

— major canal
— Allegheny Portage Railroad
◼ nuclear power plant

through hills, and bridges span rivers and valleys. All of these changes to the urban scene are examples of negative site factors being overcome.

An example of a city that grew because of political decisions is Washington, D.C. It was made the capital shortly after the Revolutionary War because it was at the center of the original 13 states of the Union. To make any other city the capital would have caused arguments among the states.

The city is at the head of the Potomac River, which was certainly a good site factor for communications. But it was also built in a swampy area that led to the spread of sickness and disease in the summer months. If Washington, D.C., had not been made the capital, bringing not only many thousands of government jobs but also encouraging places like theaters and museums to open up and be successful, negative site factors and situation would have restricted the growth of the city.

Town and Country

People live in one of two main areas: rural–small settlements or individual farms in the countryside–or urban–in a town or city. People who move from rural areas to cities (mainly to find work) are known as rural-urban migrants. Cities perform functions that give people the opportunity to work in a variety of jobs. But in rich countries many people are moving from urban areas to the countryside in search of a better quality of life. They want more space, less noise and pollution. Millions now commute into cities to work each day, which requires transportation networks with capacities undreamt of fifty years ago.

▶ Travelers at Churchgate Station, Bombay, India. Despite two suburban train systems, this huge city, India's economic center, is choked with traffic.

London, the capital city of England, shows the early importance of site factors. The Romans built the first significant settlement on the site nearly 2,000 years ago. They chose a bridging point across the Thames River (useful as a water supply, food source, and for transportation). The settlement was protected on two sides by rivers and marshland. The Romans also chose the site because it was higher than the river flood plain.

After the Romans left, the site remained attractive for development. In the 10th century the Tower of London was built and later, a few miles upstream, Westminster Abbey. The two parts of the city were separated by marsh, which was drained.

By the 14th century maps show London as the capital of England. At this point the city began to develop its range of functions. By the 19th century the city was the seat of government, a shipping and trading center, financial center, entertainment hot-spot, transportation hub, and manufacturing center.

One major function of London is its financial district, known as the City. Investments in all kinds of business are made there. This source of wealth was originally the result of a site factor: the Thames River and the resulting trade with the rest of the world. Money was needed to establish trade, and ships had to be insured. The City provided both the money and the insurance. The original site factor has been irrelevant for many years, but the City is still an important center for maritime insurance.

Following the electronic communications revolution of recent times, even the fact that this function of the city has been established for hundreds of years does not mean it will always have an advantage over other cities. Today, money can be invested or raised anywhere. This function of the city has been challenged by financial centers in other European cities such as Frankfurt in Germany.

◄ Why does Pittsburgh exist? Some of the reasons, for a city that gave the world the polio vaccine, the first petroleum refinery, and the first movie house.

Planning New Towns

As cities develop, they inevitably grow outward. The newer buildings, attractive for housing and commerce, are built on the outskirts, and the oldest buildings in the center often become neglected and overcrowded. How can this pattern be avoided?

During the Industrial Revolution in the 19th century many cities throughout the world experienced problems because of this growth. The most serious problems were the overcrowding and poor living conditions for people in the center of the city.

Origins of Modern Town Planning

Ebenezer Howard, a British town planner who had worked in London and Chicago, published a book called *Garden Cities of Tomorrow* in 1902. He was concerned about the living conditions of working-class people in city centers and the ever-increasing numbers of people moving from the country to the cities. He believed that high land costs and high-density building were at the root of the problem, and he also believed in the benefits of living in the countryside.

He proposed creating new towns to house the people living in these poor areas. The towns would be well planned, with houses laid out in traffic-free streets and with large amounts of open space. He also believed that there should be a maximum number of people (30,000) allowed to live in these new towns to avoid overcrowding.

The idea of the garden city was to provide people with a better quality of life, but without completely losing the comforts of the city. People would still have jobs, but would have pleasant surroundings and new homes to live in. By building the garden cities on cheap agricultural land outside the main city, Howard wanted to bring the countryside to the towns.

Although he produced detailed drawings of his ideas, he was not in favor of an unchanging blueprint: Every garden city was to be different and have its own character. Howard was able to persuade government and business to act on his ideas, and two garden cities were built in England during his lifetime. His ideas influenced city planning throughout the world.

Sustainable Communities

Garden cities developed in Britain, Europe, and the U.S., where today urban planning is usually intended to produce "sustainable communities," an idea that is almost the same as the earlier garden city approach. A sustainable community is one that

▶ Ebenezer Howard's "3 magnets of attraction," drawn in 1902 to show the pluses and minuses of living in different places. Howard wanted to persuade people that "Town-Country" was the most attractive option.

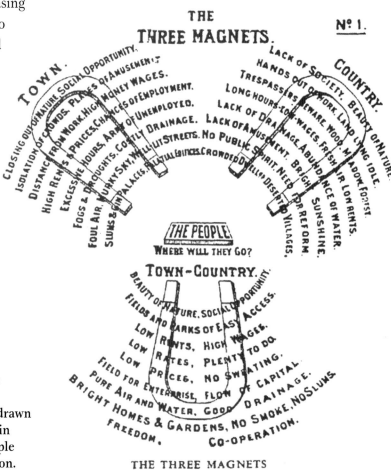

THE THREE MAGNETS

SEE ALSO: *NATIONAL MAPPING AGENCIES* 6: 10–11

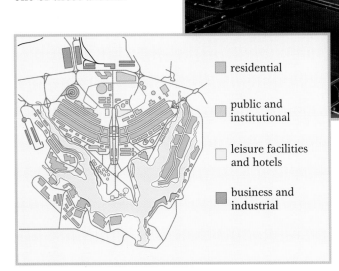

▼ ► A map and aerial photograph of Brasilia. Only a newly planned city could have such a regular and symmetrical layout. Each block in the photograph houses 2,500 people. What do you think it is like to live in one of those blocks?

residential

public and institutional

leisure facilities and hotels

business and industrial

will not grow or shrink too much over time and includes all the amenities and functions necessary for its inhabitants. Surveying and mapping the land before construction are of course the first step. The second is producing maps of the new community.

Brasilia: A South American New Town

Brasilia was built as a new town and the new capital city for the vast nation of Brazil. The site in the interior of the country was chosen in 1956, and the government moved to its new location in 1960.

The layout of Brasilia was planned to look from above like an airplane or bird. The two "wings" were to be used for housing. The main central section was zoned into areas for hotels, commerce, local government, national government, and culture. The city was built on a bare site, so everything could be planned from scratch. There were originally no traffic lights at all, the idea being that traffic would

move faster without them. (Like some other city plans, this did not work when it was tried for real.)

Expensive housing was located outside the main city next to an artificial lake. The lake was to be used for recreation. The cheaper housing was contained in "super blocks," each housing 2,500 people in ten-story apartment buildings. The idea was to create communities of people (similar to Ebenezer Howard's model) that had everything they needed. Right next to the super blocks were zones of schools, churches, and community buildings. This type of housing was provided for government workers. Surrounding the city are leisure facilities and open grasslands. Many trees were planted to improve the environment. There was very little industry planned for at all, because Brasilia was to have mainly administrative and residential functions.

To create an "instant city" like this is a difficult thing to achieve. Their inhabitants have tested older, unplanned cities over time, so that the functions of different areas have grown strongly or not at all. Not all of the expensive apartments of Brasilia are full, and *favelas*–shantytowns of squatters–stretch as far as 30 miles (50km) in all directions outside the original plan.

How Land Is Used in Cities

Cities change as time passes. They get bigger (and a very few get smaller). But that is not the only change. What happens in different parts of the city also changes. What may have been a busy industrial or manufacturing area a few decades ago might today be full of expensive luxury apartments–or it might be a wasteland. These changes can be mapped.

During the 19th century many settlements experienced rapid urban growth. This *urbanization* was linked to the growth and development of industry. Workers moved to the urban areas from rural areas in search of work. At first housing for these migrant workers would usually be close to the factories where they worked to avoid long traveling time. But as more efficient transportation systems developed, people could move farther away from their place of work. Over time, these changes create a different pattern of land use in urban areas.

Different parts of a city have different activities in them. City maps reveal these areas. Residential areas can be identified, as can retail parks, schools, and recreational open spaces. Often certain functions, such as industrial production, are in areas that are separate from the rest of the city.

If you drew a line (called a *transect*) from a city center on a map to the outskirts, you would see a number of changes in land use along it. By studying and mapping urban structure in many cities, models are developed that try to explain the land use patterns. Identifying similarities between cities can give us an understanding of the economic and social processes that give them their shape.

An Early Land Use Theory

During the 1840s the German philosopher and revolutionary Friedrich Engels wrote a book called *The Condition of the Working Classes in England.*

▼ Burgess found that Chicago in the 1920s followed the same pattern as Manchester, described 60 years earlier, but without the factory zone. The different zones are not circular because the city is on Lake Michigan.

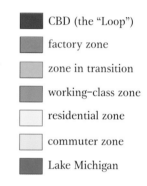

- CBD (the "Loop")
- factory zone
- zone in transition
- working–class zone
- residential zone
- commuter zone
- Lake Michigan

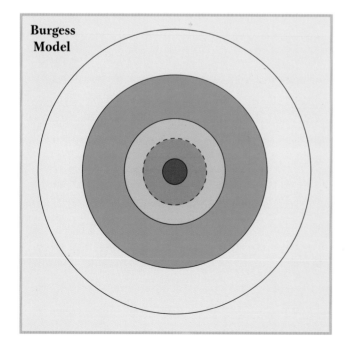

Burgess Model

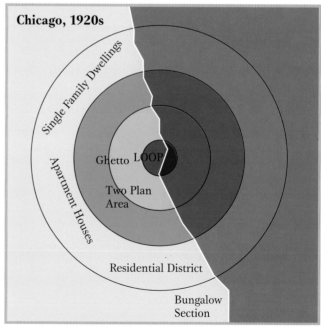

Chicago, 1920s

Single Family Dwellings

Apartment Houses

Ghetto LOOP

Two Plan Area

Residential District

Bungalow Section

SEE ALSO: *LOCATION OF CITIES AND URBAN GROWTH* **7:** *24–27*

The book was based on his experiences living and working in Manchester, England, at that time a fast-growing city full of slum housing and factories. Engels described not only the conditions of factory workers but also how the city was organized.

In the 1920s a teacher at the University of Chicago, Ernest W. Burgess, read Engels' book and compared what Engels had found in Manchester to the situation in Chicago. By comparing studies of Manchester, Chicago, and other cities, Burgess found repeated patterns of land use. He developed a theory, one that described what happened to land not just in one city, but in many cities. This theory is now called the Burgess "Concentric Zone Model."

The Burgess Model

The concentric model presents a series of rings, each of which comprises a different type of land use. The middle of the rings is the central area, known as the "Central Business District" (CBD). In this area there are department stores, large banks, offices, entertainment (bars, theaters, movies), and a variety of shops. This area of the city has good transportation facilities. Land prices are high because it is desirable for businesses to locate there.

Around the CBD is the "Zone in Transition." Land use here is mixed. The area may be run down and have poor transport networks. This part of the city is less desirable for large stores and other facilities. It consists mainly of older and overcrowded housing along with less impressive offices, plus warehouses and some small-scale industry. Poor people live there. Housing is usually quite cheap because of its low quality. Ethnic minorities sometimes make up the bulk of the population.

The "Zone of Working Men's Homes" contains housing built for people who have moved out of the Zone in Transition. The people living there take advantage of still

The City of Sunderland

The maps of Sunderland (a city in the northeast of England) show changing land use from 1971 to 1996. The built-up areas of the city expand into areas that were agricultural land. The maps show the increasing need for new housing. The original concentration of housing and roads near the coast was built when Sunderland was an important center of ship-building and heavy industry. This industry has declined from the 1970s. The central business district is located to the south of the river. The best housing is located to the very south of the city away from the industry. The old, poorer housing is located next to the river, where the old industry was located. New housing is to the west. The city has followed the Burgess model in several ways, but the locations of the sea and the river have distorted the ring pattern.

► Land use 1971; most housing is close to the docks.

▼ Land use 1996; farm-land becomes residential and urban green area.

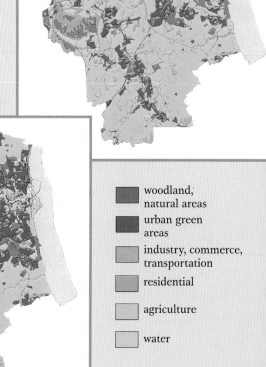

■ woodland, natural areas

■ urban green areas

■ industry, commerce, transportation

■ residential

■ agriculture

■ water

relatively low rents and an effective transportation network to get to work. All cities grow outward as housing and transportation develop side-by-side.

The "Residential Zone" is an area of higher-quality housing for the wealthier city dwellers. Houses are larger, and there is more open space. Housing is *low density*–there are fewer houses per unit of land. Today in modern cities these areas have retail parks and office developments mixed in with the housing.

The "Commuter Zone" is the area beyond the edge of the city. Land use there has changed from farmland to housing and leisure facilities. The urban area eats into the surrounding countryside. High rates of car ownership have allowed this growth, and the residents can take advantage of this and the cheaper cost of land to live on bigger properties.

Changing Land Use over Time

Maps are the ideal way of showing changing patterns of land use over time. They can also help us see whether a city follows the Burgess model, has slight variations from it, or has grown in a completely different way.

New York City: Mapping Out the Problems

Maps can show the true character of cities by mapping features other than buildings and space. Mapping of statistics such as income levels reveals areas of poverty and areas in need of new development. Armed with a detailed set of these thematic maps, city planners can identify and tackle urban problems. What has happened to New York City over the last 20 years is an example of this kind of planning.

New York City is situated on Manhattan Island, Staten Island, and parts of nearby Long Island and the shores of the Hudson River at its mouth. Being situated on islands has molded the communications network of the city. Today it is the biggest city in the U.S., and more than 18 million people live in the

conurbation (the urban area) centered on New York City itself but including urban areas that have built up around it.

There have been many changes in land use in the city over the years. The city's population is actually falling. In the Bronx, for example, there are 40% fewer people than 50 years ago. Many people have moved beyond the edge of the city in search of a better quality of life.

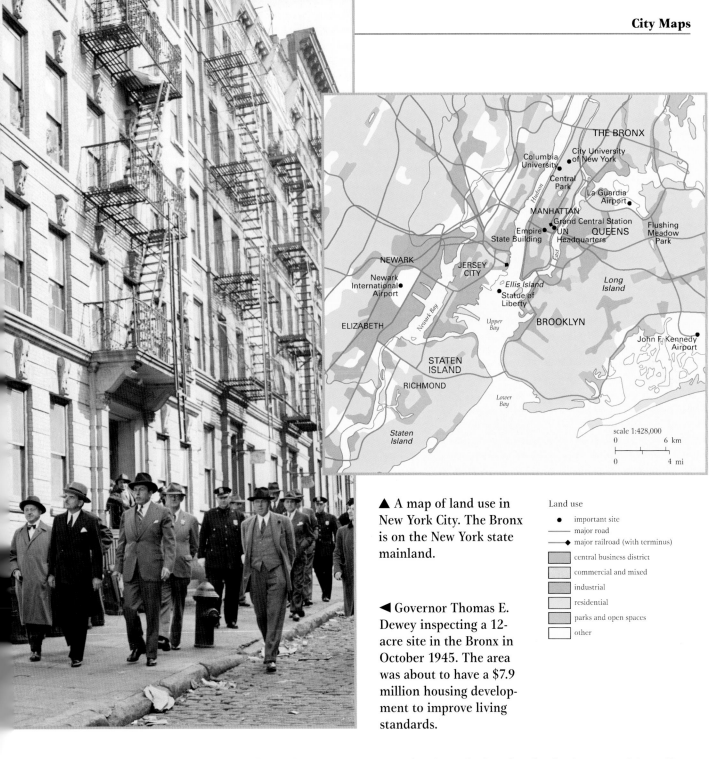

▲ A map of land use in New York City. The Bronx is on the New York state mainland.

Land use

- ● important site
- — major road
- ◆ major railroad (with terminus)
- ▮ central business district
- ▯ commercial and mixed
- ▮ industrial
- ▯ residential
- ▮ parks and open spaces
- ▯ other

◄ Governor Thomas E. Dewey inspecting a 12-acre site in the Bronx in October 1945. The area was about to have a $7.9 million housing development to improve living standards.

New York City planners have tried to solve problems of poor housing and deprived neighborhoods in two ways. First, they have encouraged new growth at the city edge. This has meant building on much of the open space around the city. The second method has been to improve things in the city center to encourage people to stay. The planners have tried to regenerate open spaces and improve leisure or recreation facilities.

Reduction of crime levels also has a positive effect on the inner city. Thematic mapping can indicate improvements in crime figures over time.

Maps are essential to plan this kind of urban renewal. But they are not just maps that show where the parks are: They are maps that show things like ethnic background of residents, birth rates, income levels, daily movement of commuters, and emigration from the city.

Urban Transportation Maps

The city traveler needs certain kinds of information from a map if he is using the public transportation system. While some cities do cover huge areas—cities like Los Angeles or Brasilia—distance from one place to another is not the main thing he or she needs to know. Where to get on and where to get off is usually more important.

Many cities have systems of public transportation that use underground railroads. This causes a problem for the cartographer. It is vital that a map of the subway be easy to read and understand, not just for the city dweller but for the visitor who may have no idea of distance or direction. Yet the subway can give him or her no visual clues that can be linked to the map. The efficient running of big cities like New York, Tokyo, and London that have millions of commuters and visitors relies heavily on clear mapping of public transportation.

Location, Not Distance

The usual solution is to create a *topological* subway map. This type of mapping is really like an electrical circuit diagram because, like the diagram, it does not show things to scale, and it uses symbols. The most important facts to show are the positions of subway stations relative to each other: In New York the Fifth Avenue Station is the stop between Times Square Station and Grand Central Station. That is what the traveler needs to know. The true distance between each of the stations is not really important. So subway maps are not drawn true to scale, but instead they stretch and reduce distances to make the map more readable and more compact.

The top map opposite is part of the topological underground railway map of London (the subway in London is called "the underground" or, sometimes, "the tube"). The map shows the underground lines and the location of the main stations. The tracks are drawn as straight lines with few curves, and the whole system can be easily shown on one map that could fit inside your pocket. But the central area of the map is "stretched." The actual distances between the stations are quite short. And in comparison the map makes distances between stations in the suburbs look much shorter than they really are. The real tracks are not straight lines, and they even sometimes go uphill and downhill. You cannot tell that from the map. The lower map shows the accurate, to-scale location of some of the stations and track direction for comparison.

Subway maps are produced without any scale. Because travelers can't see the features on the ground, they do not need to know all the properly scaled details; underground, there isn't much to see anyway! The idea of simplifying the routes of subways and underground railways has been extended to all forms of transportation: Many bus maps also use topological mapping techniques.

▲ Topological subway map provided by the Washington Metropolitan Area Transit Authority. Different colors identify individual lines.

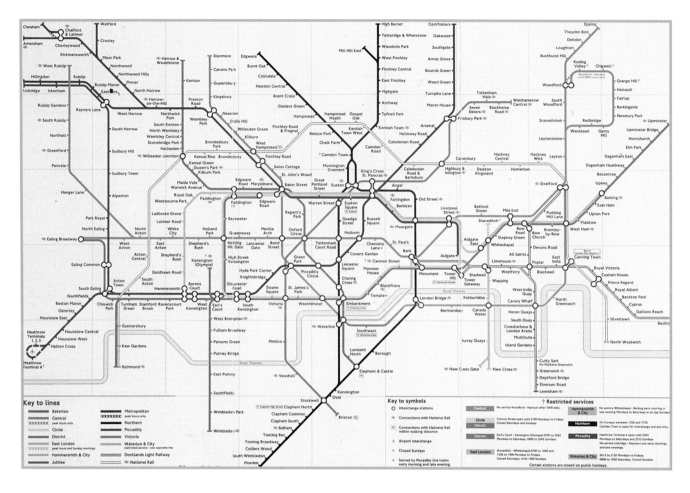

▲ A topological map of the London underground. This map is designed for clarity and user-friendliness. Station locations do not relate to each other in the same way in reality (see below).

▶ A topographic map of actual station locations for a section of the map above. Information about features on the surface–roads and parks–is included. Follow the different rail lines to locate the same stations on both maps.

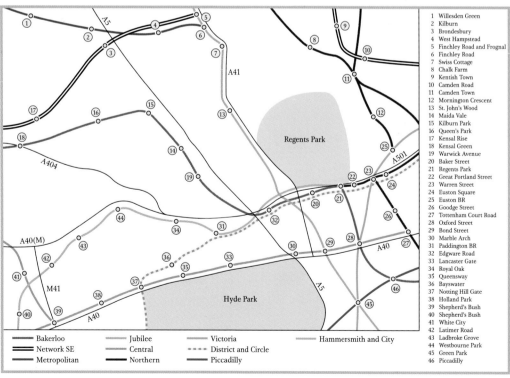

1	Willesden Green
2	Kilburn
3	Brondesbury
4	West Hampstead
5	Finchley Road and Frognal
6	Finchley Road
7	Swiss Cottage
8	Chalk Farm
9	Kentish Town
10	Camden Road
11	Camden Town
12	Mornington Crescent
13	St. John's Wood
14	Maida Vale
15	Kilburn Park
16	Queen's Park
17	Kensal Rise
18	Kensal Green
19	Warwick Avenue
20	Baker Street
21	Regents Park
22	Great Portland Street
23	Warren Street
24	Euston Square
25	Euston BR
26	Goodge Street
27	Tottenham Court Road
28	Oxford Street
29	Bond Street
30	Marble Arch
31	Paddington BR
32	Edgware Road
33	Lancaster Gate
34	Royal Oak
35	Queensway
36	Bayswater
37	Notting Hill Gate
38	Holland Park
39	Shepherd's Bush
40	Shepherd's Bush
41	White City
42	Latimer Road
43	Ladbroke Grove
44	Westbourne Park
45	Green Park
46	Piccadilly

City Tourist Guides

Go to any city and try to find your way around. If you have never been there before, the task is difficult. A specialized form of mapping is there to help: the tourist map.

Walk around the streets of an unfamiliar city. What might you notice? Perhaps open spaces, parks, and roads or large buildings, shops, and restaurants; maybe statues and monuments. The tourist cartographer has to decide which of these to include. A list of the main tourist attractions of the city plotted onto a street map might provide the necessary information, but would tourists actually be able to use it? There are a number of further changes that can make the map more "user-friendly."

A good starting point is to make the streets on the map wider than they actually are relative to the buildings. This lets the mapmaker add details like road names, transportation routes, and landmarks more clearly. Pictures can highlight individual buildings. Tourist maps tend to rely more on pictures than on symbols. By using sketches that look like the buildings, even poor map readers can find out where they are by recognizing what is around them.

The map may also help in finding locations by supplying lettered and numbered grid squares (for example, the museum is in square E4). A list of places and streets, known as a gazetteer, lists the grid references for the most popular destinations. At popular tourist sites a large poster version of

▲ Many cities have large tourist information maps in popular areas.

◄ Consulting a tourist map of the layout of the ruins of the Acropolis in Athens, Greece. The map is an oblique view to show height of buildings.

▲ Tourist guides in various languages to the city of Istanbul, Turkey.

SEE ALSO: *PILGRIMS AND THE FIRST TOURISTS* 3: 8–9

the tourist map can often be found on a noticeboard, with a "YOU ARE HERE" arrow. It lets the visitors orient themselves with their surroundings. As with most kinds of map, including those that we have looked at in this book–pictorial maps, panoramic maps, even axonometric maps–knowing where you are on the map is the first step to using it.

New Technology

When finding your way in the city, you no longer have to take a paper map with you. Maps are available from in-car navigation systems, through palm PCs, and cellphones. Early in-car navigation systems from the 1980s relied on CDs that held information about an area in the form of a map. The driver would indicate to the computer where the car was at the start of the journey, the correct CD map was found, and the position was highlighted on the screen. Sensors on the car wheels, measuring speed and distance, would then transmit information to the computer so it could track the car's position.

Today, Global Positioning System (GPS) satellites can locate your car's position. The computer software is also more sophisticated, sometimes able to give a "best guess" of position if the car cannot receive the GPS signal–in a narrow city street or in a tunnel, for example. Drivers can now use the system to plot an alternative route to avoid traffic jams. The type of map provided by these systems is similar to a tourist map because it shows a simplified street pattern, highlights important landmarks, and only includes the most vital information for navigation.

For the tourist, as well as route planning, most navigation computer software allows you to select further information that you want to include on your map. It could be accommodation, tourist attractions, landmarks, or detailed route plan notes.

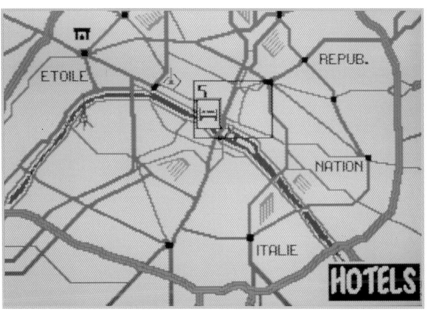

▲ **CARMINAT car navigation display of central Paris. CARMINAT is linked to the SIRIUS traffic monitoring system to help avoid traffic jams.**

Tourist maps are available on the Internet. Practically any city or tourist area you care to visit has a web page, complete with a tourist guide map, so you can plan your trip in advance.

Are These Maps Really New?

These maps are actually an updated electronic version of old route maps. Coaching maps (showing the routes of horse-drawn carriages that you could catch just like a bus) were produced for the 17th-century traveler. They only included the road and features on either side. The reasoning was that you only needed on the map what you could see from the road. The maps were sometimes produced on thin strips of paper that could be unwound and read like a scroll. They included distances between places, important road junctions, and landmarks.

The aims of the 17th-century mapmaker and the Internet cartographer are the same–to give travelers as much information as they need without giving too much confusing detail–but the way of delivering that information is very different.

Glossary

Words in *italics* have their own entries in the glossary

Aerial photograph (or air photograph) – a photograph looking straight down at the earth, taken from an airplane

Agrimensores – Roman land surveyors who worked in the towns and on military campaigns throughout the Roman Empire

Axonometric maps – maps showing three-dimensional objects so that the scale for each object is the same whether close up or in the distance. Building heights, for example, can be compared right across the area mapped; this cannot be done with the alternative display method, *perspective* viewing, in which objects appear smaller the farther away they are

Aztecs – a people who in the 15th and early 16th century ruled a large empire in what is now central and southern Mexico; they probably came from the northern Mexico plateau in the 12th century

Base map – a map that shows base data, fundamental cartographic information such as political boundaries and topography. (*See* Topographic map)

Bearing – the direction someone is heading measured as an angle away from north; due north has a bearing of 0 degrees, while due west has a bearing of 270 degrees. Bearing is also sometimes used to describe angular position or direction in relation to any two known points

Bird's-eye view – a straight-down view of the earth

Cadastral system – a method of recording ownership of land based on registers, legal documents, and maps showing the boundaries of individual tracts

CBD – the central business district of a large city where commerce, government, and other important activities take place

Cholera – a water-borne disease; symptoms include sickness and diarrhea, which can lead to death if untreated

City-state – a city powerful and rich enough to run its own affairs more or less independent of a central national government. Ancient city-states like Athens and city-states of the Middle Ages such as Venice were like small countries

Commuters – workers who live some distance away from their place of work and must use transportation systems such as railways and buses, or their cars, every working day

Compass – an instrument showing the direction of *magnetic north* using a magnetic needle; *bearing* can be calculated by using a compass

Concentric – describes a series of circles one inside the other focused on the same point

Contour – an imaginary line connecting places in the landscape that are at equal height above (or below) sea level. The distance of contour lines from each other on a map shows how steeply or gradually land rises

Delta – the area at the mouth of some rivers where the main stream breaks up into smaller rivulets

Epidemiology – the study of how disease spreads

Favelas – a settlement of shacks or semipermanent shelters lying on the outskirts of a city, usually in South America (*see also* Squatter settlements)

Forbidden City – The imperial palace within the inner city of Beijing, China. The 9,000 rooms inside housed the emperor and imperial court from 1421 to 1911. It was called the Forbidden City because no commoner or foreigner could enter without permission from court officials

Functions – the different aspects of a city that make it work; the services offered by an urban settlement, including opportunities for work, entertainment, investment, shelter, and so on

Gazetteer – a list of names of places, with location specified; often accompanied by a map

Global Positioning System (GPS) – a system of 24 satellites orbiting the earth and sending out highly accurate radio signals indicating where they are; a GPS receiver held by someone on the earth can interpret the signals and calculate the receiver's position on earth

Grid squares – *See* Grid system

Grid system – uses a mesh of horizontal and vertical lines over the face of a map to pinpoint the position of places. The mesh of lines often helps show distance of locations east and north from a set position. The zero point can be any convenient location and is often the bottom-left corner of the map

Groma – a land surveying instrument used by Roman *agrimensores* to set out right angles on the ground

Incas – South American Indians who ruled an empire along the Pacific coast and in the Andean Highlands at the time of the Spanish conquest in 1532. They built a vast network of roads throughout their empire, and their architecture was advanced. But they kept no written records. Machu Picchu in the Andes Mountains of south central Peru is one of their fortress cities

Industrial Revolution – the period of history (in the late 18th and 19th centuries) when some societies that had been mainly agricultural were transformed into manufacturing economies, using coal and steam power to run factories and transport goods

Internet – the network of interconnected computers throughout the world linked by wires and satellites and running software to allow them to communicate with each other

Land use – how human beings use land, for example, for housing, agriculture, or recreation. Land use is different from land cover, which describes the natural vegetation or environment in an area, for example, forest, desert, or ice cap

Layer tinting – a design used for showing height of mountains and hills on a map using bands of color to define zones where the land is between two height values (between 100 and 250 meters above sea level, for example)

Low Density – density is an expression of the number of items per unit area. For example, a low-density housing area would mean that there are fewer houses per unit of land than in a built-up area

Magnetic north – the northerly direction in the earth's magnetic field, indicated by the direction in which a compass needle points

Mayans – a people who created a vast and sophisticated civilization in what is now southern Mexico, Guatemala, and northern Belize. At its height, from about 250 A.D. to 900 A.D., Mayan culture created more than 40 cities with populations ranging from 5,000 to 50,000. The Mayans built huge stone buildings and pyramid temples, and—unlike the *Incas*—had a written language

Morphology – the overall shape and structure of a city; but also of the land or any other feature

Oblique view – a view of the earth's surface from above, not looking straight down but at an angle to the surface

Optical perspective – geometrical scientific laws about how light reaches the eye from any viewpoint; followed when making *oblique* maps (*see also* Perspective)

Orientate – to position a map or surveying instrument, or a person, with reference to known features or to the points of the *compass*. The word comes from the Latin *oriens*, which means rising and refers to the sun, which rises in the east. So "the Orient" came to mean countries east of the Mediterranean

Panorama – a wide *oblique* view, showing an area of countryside or the extent of a city

Perspective – a method of showing three-dimensional objects graphically in such a way that they look natural, as they would in the real world; objects appear to be smaller the farther away they are

Philanthropist – someone who shows concern for others through charitable acts; often refers to rich people who use their money for good causes

Pictorial map – a map that uses small pictures to represent buildings and other important landmarks

Portage – the carrying of small boats or their cargo overland between two navigable waterways

Relief – the shape of the earth's surface, its hills, mountains, and depressions

Sanitation – protection of health through hygiene, preventing infections and epidemics

Scale – the ratio of the size of a map to the area of the real world that it represents

Situation – a settlement's location in relation to the surrounding land and features and other settlements

Squatter settlements – informal areas of housing, like *favelas*, on the edge of many third-world cities. People who have moved from other places, often the countryside, gather there to settle

Theodolite – a surveying instrument used to figure out the angle between two points on the earth's surface viewed from a third point

Topographic map – a map that shows natural features such as hills, rivers, and forests, and man-made features such as roads and buildings

Topological maps – maps that show relationships among objects but are not necessarily to scale like a *topographic map*. A topological subway map, for example, shows the sequence of the stations—their relationship along the railroad line—but not the actual distances between them

Transect – a line drawn across an area or a map that is used to sample varying characteristics, such as land use

Urban – describes built-up areas of human settlement; towns and cities

Urbanization – the growth of a settlement so that it gradually comes to resemble a town or city

Further Reading and Websites

Barber, Peter, ed. *The Lie of the Land*, British Library Publishing, 2001

Driver, Cline *Early American Maps and Views*, University Press of Virginia, 1988

Forte, I., et al., *Map Skills and Geography: Inventive Exercises to Sharpen Skills and Raise Achievement*, Incentive Publications, 1998

Haywood, John, et al., *Atlas of World History*, Barnes & Noble Books, 2001

Letham, Lawrence *GPS Made Easy*, Rocky Mountain Books, 1998

Monmonier, Mark *How to Lie with Maps*, University of Chicago Press, 1991

Monmonier, Mark *Map Appreciation*, Prentice Hall, 1988

Meltzer, M. *Columbus and the World around Him*, Franklin Watts, 1990

Stefoff, Rebecca *Young Oxford Companion to Maps and Mapmaking*, Oxford University Press, 1995

Thrower, Norman J. W. *Maps and Civilization: Cartography in Culture and Society*, 2nd ed., University of Chicago Press, 1999

Wilford, John. N. *The Mapmakers*, Pimlico, 2002

www.auslig.gov.au/
National mapping division of Australia. Find an aerial photograph of any area of the country

http://cgdi.gc.ca/ccatlas/atlas.htm
Internet-based Canadian Communities Atlas project. Schools create their own atlas

www.earthamaps.com/
Search by place name for U.S. city maps, with zoom facility

http://earthtrends.wri.org
World Resources Institute mapping of energy resources, agriculture, forestry, government, climate, and other thematic maps

http://geography.about.com
Links to pages on cartography, historic maps, GIS, and GPS; print out blank and outline maps for study purposes

http://ihr.sas.ac.uk/maps/
History of cartography; no images, but search for links to many other cartographic topics

www.lib.utexas.edu/maps/
Vast map collection at the University of Texas, historical and modern, including maps produced by the CIA

www.lib.virginia.edu/exhibits/lewis_clark/
Information on historic expeditions, including Lewis and Clark

www.lindahall.org/pubserv/hos/stars/
Exhibition of the Golden Age of the celestial atlas, 1482–1851

www.LivGenMI.com/1895.htm
A U.S. atlas first printed in 1895. Search for your town, city, or county

http://memory.loc.gov/ammem/gmdhtml/
Map collections 1500–1999, the Library of Congress; U.S. maps, including military campaigns and exploration

www.nationalgeographic.com/education/maps_geography/
The National Geographic educational site

http://oddens.geog.uu.nl/index.html
15,500 cartographic links; search by country or keyword

www.ordsvy.gov.uk/
Site of one of the oldest national mapping agencies. Search for and download historical and modern mapping of the U.K. Go to Understand Mapping page for cartographic glossary

www.mapzone.co.uk/
Competitions and quizzes for younger readers about Great Britain; site run by Ordnance Survey

http://www.libs.uga.edu/darchive/hargrett/maps/maps.html
University of Georgia historical map collection; maps from the 16th to the early 20th century

http://topozone.com/
Search by place name or latitude and longitude for all areas of the U.S. Maps at various scales

www.un.org/Depts/Cartographic/english/htmain.htm
United Nations cartographic section. Search by country and by different UN missions worldwide

http://mapping.usgs.gov/
U.S. national atlas and much more, including satellite images

http://interactive2.usgs.gov/learningweb/students/homework_geography.asp
USGS site for students; all kinds of useful information. Create your own map by plotting latitude and longitude coordinates

www.worldatlas.com/
World atlas and lots of statistics about all countries of the world

Set Index

Numbers in **bold** in this index refer to the volume number. They are followed by the relevant page numbers. A page number in *italics* indicates an illustration.

Picture Credits

Abbreviation: C   Corbis

Jacket images Oblique view of antique map (background), Ken Reid/Telegraph Colour Library/Getty Images; T-in-O map of the world drawn in 1450 (inset, top), AKG London; three-dimensional map of the topography of Mars (inset, bottom), NASA/Science Photo Library. **6** Robert Harding Picture Library; **7** Yann Arthus-Bertrand/C; **11l** Ancient Art & Architecture Collection; **11r** The British Library; **12** Scala Group S.p.A.; **13** Liverpool University Library; **14l** Bettmann/C; **14b** Gianni Dagli Orti/C; **15** Guildhall Library, London; **16** Paul Almasy/C; **16-17** Joseph Sohm; Chromo Sohm Inc./C; **18-19** Ludington Limited; **19** Charles E. Rotkin/C; **20-21** Hulton/ Archive; **22-23** The British Library; **27** Robert Holmes/C; **28** diagram from *Tomorrow a Peaceful Path to Real Reform* by Ebenezer Howard; **29** Yann Arthus-Bertrand/C; **31** Newcastle University/European Union; **32-33** Bettmann/C; **34** Washington Metropolitan Area/Transit Authority; **35** London Transport Museum; **36t** Bob Krist/C; **36bl** Farrell Grehan/C; **36br** David Samuel Robbins/C; **37** Philippe Plailly/Eurelios/Science Photo Library.

While every effort has been made to trace the copyright holders of illustrations reproduced in this book, the publishers will be pleased to rectify any omissions or inaccuracies.